THE VALUE OF BELIEVING IN YOURSELF

The Story of Louis Pasteur

VALUE COMMUNICATIONS, INC.
PUBLISHERS
LA JOLLA, CALIFORNIA

THE
VALUE OF
BELIEVING IN
YOURSELF

The Story of
Louis Pasteur

BY SPENCER JOHNSON, M.D.

The Value of Believing in Yourself is part of the ValueTales series.

The ValueTale of Louis Pasteur Text copyright © 1976 by
Spencer Johnson, M.D. Illustrations copyright © 1976 by Value
Communications, Inc.

Second Edition
Manufactured in the United States of America
For information write to: Value Tales, P.O. Box 1012
La Jolla, CA 92038

Library of Congress Cataloging in Publication Data

Johnson, Spencer.
    The value of believing in yourself.

    First ed. published in 1975 under title: The ValueTale of
Louis Pasteur.
    SUMMARY: Retells the story of Louis Pasteur, whose
unwavering belief in the concept of germs led to a cure for
rabies.
    1.   Pasteur, Louis, 1822-1895—Juvenile literature.
2.   Self-reliance—Juvenile literature.
3.   Bacteriologists—France—Biography—Juvenile literature.
[1.   Pasteur, Louis, 1822-1895.   2.   Scientists.
3.   Self-reliance]   I.   Pileggi, Steve.   II.   Title.
QR31.P37J63   1976   591.2′3′220924 [B]
[92]   76-55225
ISBN 0-916392-06-6

This tale is about a person who believed in himself, Louis Pasteur. The story that follows is based on events in his life. More historical facts about Louis Pasteur can be found on page 61.

Once upon a time...

in far-off France, there lived a man named Louis Pasteur.

Now and then this man, who was a doctor of science, would put on his tall black hat and his bright orange coat and walk in the park.

"I believe I can. I believe I can," he would say to himself as he went along.

What do you think it was that Louis Pasteur believed he could do?

It was something important—so important that Louis Pasteur didn't even notice the other people in the park.

"I must find the invisible enemy," said he. "I must find the Rabies germs that hide inside people and make them sick—so sick that they die."

"Once I find that invisible enemy, I'll think of a way to kill it. Then sick people will be well again."

Louis Pasteur sat on a bench and thought about that invisible enemy. "I just *know* I can do it," he said.

"What a silly man." said some children who happened to be near. "If an enemy is invisible, that means no one can see it. If no one can see it, no one can find it."

Louis Pasteur pretended that he didn't hear those nosy children. He hurried to his laboratory on Ulm Street in Paris, where he worked everyday.

RUE D'ULM
←

Some of the children followed him. So did some grownups who wanted to know what he was doing. They peeped through the laboratory window.

"You'll never do it!" they shouted. "No one can find an invisible enemy!"

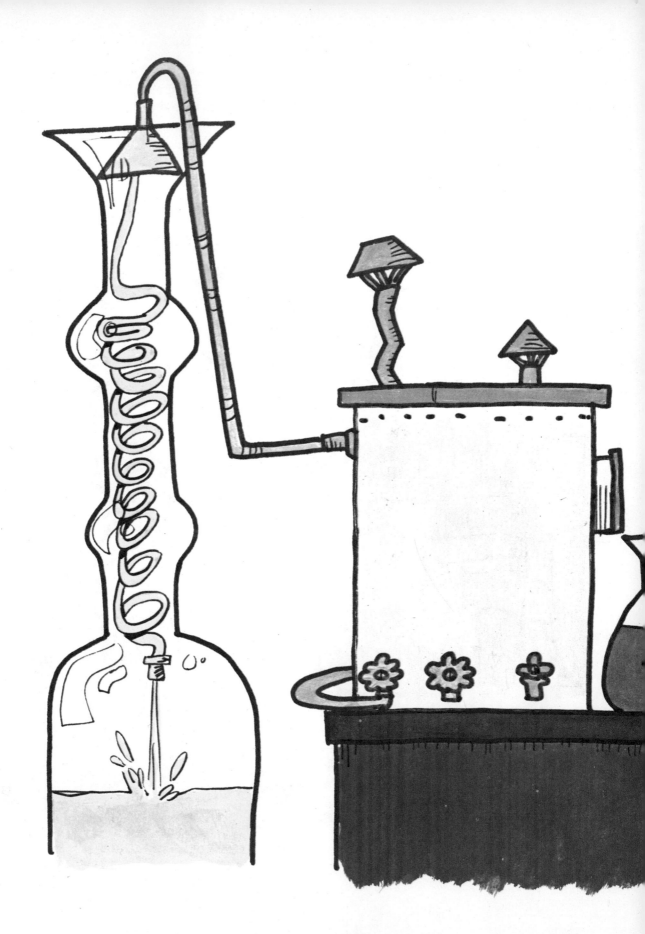

Louis Pasteur didn't care what the children thought. He didn't care what the grownups thought, either. He believed in *himself*.

"I know I'm right," he said. "I'm sure I can do it."

So, because he believed in himself, he kept on working. He kept on *doing* what he thought was right.

It was hard work, but Louis Pasteur was happy. He knew that if he did find the invisible enemy—the Rabies germs—he could help many sick people to be well again.

While the mean children laughed and poked fun at Louis Pasteur who was working in his laboratory in France, a little boy was laughing and poking a stick at a poor, sick dog in another land far away—a land called Germany.

The boy's name was Joey. He wasn't really a cruel little boy. He was just thoughtless, as children sometimes are, and he liked to tease, as children sometimes do.

Soon Joey could see that the dog was very mad. He even had white foam around his mouth—foam like whipped cream. He tried to bark, as if to say, "Stop it! Stop it!" But he couldn't bark.

Something was wrong!

Do you know what was wrong?

Suppose you could look inside that dog with a great magnifying glass, or a microscope. What would you see?

That's right! You'd see the invisible enemy—the rabies germs that were making the dog so sick.

The dog was so sick and so mad that he would bite at anything—even at the rocks or the trees.

If he could, he would surely bite the boy who had poked a stick at him.

When Joey went off, he didn't notice one very important thing.

Can you see what that thing was?

Yes, it was the gate. The gate in the fence had come open. The mad, sick dog could get out. He could run after Joey and bite him.

That's exactly what the dog did.

"Ouch! Ouch!" cried Joey, as the mad, sick dog bit him on the arms and the legs.

And then it happened! The invisible enemy—the rabies germs that were hiding in the dog—traveled from the dog's foaming mouth into the little boy.

"Help! Help!" Joey shouted. "Daddy! Please help me!"

Joey's father heard, and he ran out of his cottage to see what was the matter.

When he saw the dog biting his little boy, he was terribly afraid. Yes, he was a big, strong man, but he was afraid. Sometimes even daddies are afraid.

But Joey's father was brave. He ran toward the dog.
"Get away! Get away!" he shouted at the dog. He
waved his arms and stamped his feet.

The dog ran off.

Joey's father chased the dog back through the gate. When the dog was safely behind the fence, Joey's father carefully closed the gate.

But the damage had already been done.

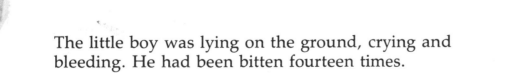

The little boy was lying on the ground, crying and bleeding. He had been bitten fourteen times.

"I'm afraid my boy is going to be very sick," said Joey's father to himself.

His father picked Joey up. "Did you tease that dog?" he asked.

"Yes, Daddy, and I'm sorry," whispered Joey. He was badly hurt and he felt very tired.

"I'll take you home," said his father sadly. He was sad because he knew the terrible thing that had happened to his son.

The little boy now had the invisible enemy—the
Rabies germs—hiding inside him. Soon he was not
only hurt and tired, he was sick.

Everyone who knew Joey was sad. Everyone knew
that if a person was bitten by a sick, mad dog, that
person would surely die.

Before long the sick dog died.

It was very quiet in Joey's home. His parents did
not know how to help Joey. They could only wait.

Then, one day, there was news. Joey's mother saw it first, and she shouted for joy. "Wonderful! Wonderful!" she cried.

How could she think *anything* was wonderful when her little boy was dying? What do you think she had read in the newspaper?

31

"A doctor of science has found a way to save people like Joey!" she said. "He says sick people like Joey have been invaded by an invisible enemy. He has found the enemy and he has also found a way to kill it!"

Do you know who the man was?

Of course! It was Louis Pasteur, the man who believed in himself. He had known he was right, and he had done what he set out to do.

"Father, we'll need a carriage," said Joey's mother. "We must take Joey to Paris, to see Dr. Louis Pasteur. Perhaps he can save Joey's life."

Joey's father ran. He hired a fine carriage and a stout and able coachman. Six fast white horses were hitched to the carriage.

Joey's parents wrapped Joey up in warm, soft blankets and put him into the carriage.

"I wish the dog hadn't died," said Joey sadly. "At least, I wish I hadn't poked that dog with a stick."

"Let's go!" shouted the coachman. "We haven't a second to lose!"

"Hurry!" said Joey's mother, as the horses galloped down the long, long road to Paris.

"Hurry!" pleaded Joey's father.

Even the trees beside the road seemed to whisper, "Hurry! Hurry! Faster! Faster!"

They were tired and dusty when they arrived at
Louis Pasteur's door, but they were happy to be
there. They knocked, and Louis Pasteur opened the
door and welcomed them.

"Dr. Pasteur," said the mother as she smiled a brave smile. "We have come a long way to see you. Our little boy was bitten by a mad dog, and he's very sick. Can you help us?"

"Perhaps," said Louis Pasteur. "I have found a way to kill the invisible enemy—those rabies germs that hide inside of sick animals. Perhaps I can kill the ones that are hidden in your little boy."

"I have invented a Vaccine," explained Louis Pasteur. "In my Vaccine are Magical Soldiers with bright eyes that can see in the dark. When they see the invisible enemy inside of Joey, my Magical Soldiers, who are very strong, will kill that enemy."

Joey had been put into bed. When he heard Louis Pasteur say this, he rose up a little. "Dr. Pasteur," he said, "do you mean your Magical Soldiers will be inside of *me*?"

"Yes," said Louis Pasteur.

Joey looked puzzled.
"But how will they get there?"

"Very easily," said Louis Pasteur. "My Magical Soldiers can march through long needles and into little boys. They march together, like a mighty army."

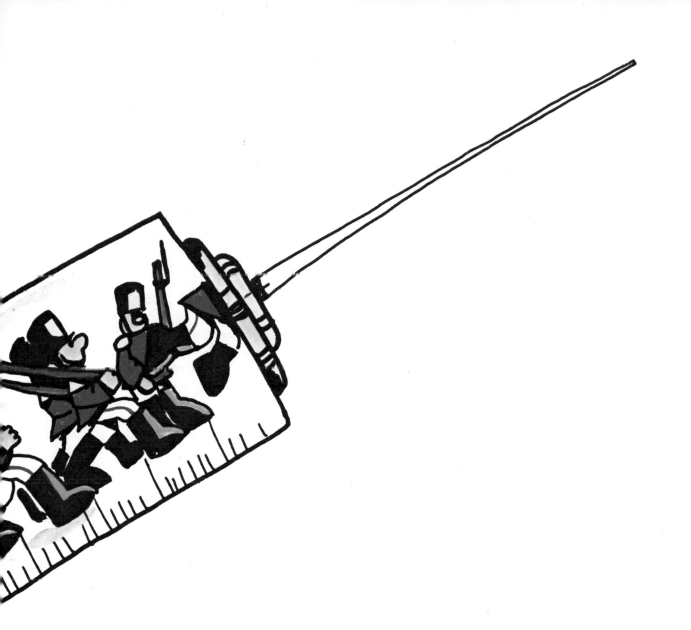

"But needles hurt," said Joey.

"Sometimes," admitted Dr. Pasteur. "But can you be brave, Joey, while my Magical Soldiers march into you?"

"I'll be very brave," promised Joey.

"Then you will be the very first person to have a shot of my Rabies Vaccine," said Louis Pasteur.

This worried Joey's father. "The very first person?" he wondered. "Will it be dangerous? Are you sure your Vaccine will work on a little boy?"

"I believe it will," said Louis Pasteur, and he gave Joey his shot.

The Magical Soldiers marched into the little boy.

When they got inside Joey, they found that it was
dark. The Magical Soldiers peered here and there
with their magical eyes. At last they spotted the
enemy—those Rabies germs that had always been
invisible, until now.

At first they saw only twelve. Can you see them,
too?

They knew that there were really millions of germs
inside Joey.

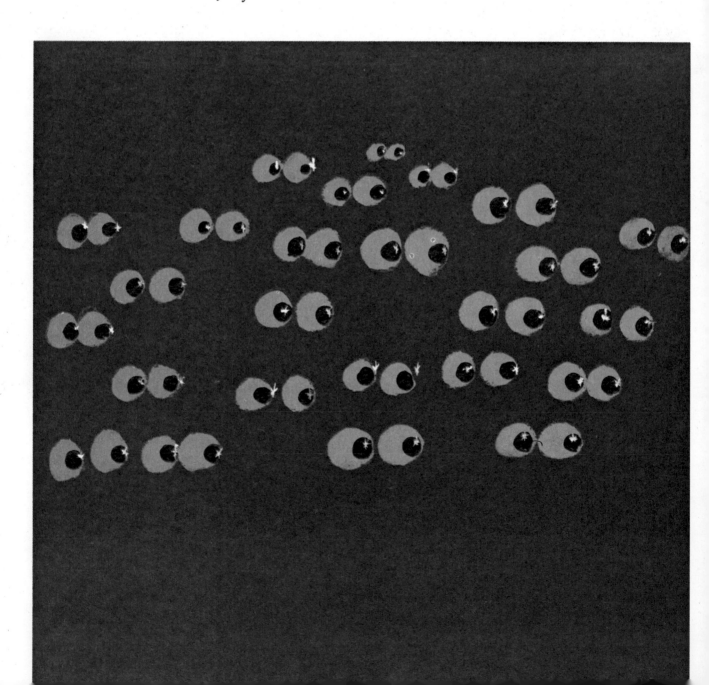

"You'll never beat us!" said the Terrible Germs.

"Yes, we will," cried the Magical Soldiers.

The battle began. The Magical Soldiers attacked the invisible enemy and fought bravely.

It wasn't very comfortable for Joey. Would you be comfortable if you had an army of Magical Soldiers fighting a war inside you?

But as the Soldiers in the Rabies Vaccine killed more and more of the enemy, Joey felt better and better.

When the last of the enemy had been beaten, Joey felt well—so well that he jumped out of bed and danced around in a circle with his mother, his father, and of course with Dr. Louis Pasteur, who felt as much like dancing as any of them.

"Hurrah! Hurrah!" they all shouted.

Then Joey thanked Louis Pasteur and rode back
home to Germany in the carriage with his mother
and father.

In Joey's village the people lined the streets. They
laughed and waved to Joey. Everyone was so happy
that he was alive. Even the yellow sun in the sky
seemed happy.

Above the rooftops, the village bells rang out a joyful tune. They seemed to be singing, "Safe! Safe! Now everyone is safe! No one has to die of Rabies!"

Meanwhile, back in France where he lived and worked, many people now wanted to talk to Dr. Pasteur.

"Dr. Pasteur," said some of the children, "we think you are wonderful. You found the cure for Rabies."

"Yes, I did," smiled Dr. Pasteur. "And I am very happy. But do you know what made me feel so good while I was trying to find the cure?"

"When I was working in my laboratory," Dr. Pasteur said, "I enjoyed the times when I believed in myself. In those days, I didn't always succeed. But even if I didn't, it always felt good to believe that I could."

As you can see, our story ends happily. And now perhaps you might like to think about *yourself*.

Of course, what you may decide to do in your *own* life may be very different indeed! But whatever you choose for yourself, let's hope it will make *you* happier . . .

Just like our good friend, Louis Pasteur.

The End

LOUIS PASTEUR
1822-1895

Louis Pasteur was born in Dole, in the Province of Dura, France, in 1822. As a chemist, and later as a bacteriologist, Pasteur did more than any other man of his time to further medical progress. However, because he was not a physician, many medical men of the 1800's jeered at his theories. He ignored their scorn because he believed so strongly that bacteria, or germs, did indeed exist and that they could cause disease. He continued to work in his own way, having faith in himself, and eventually discovered the cure for a silkworm disease, for anthrax and for rabies.

Pasteur also invented a process to keep milk from spoiling. It consisted of heating the milk to 140°F for thirty minutes, then cooling it quickly and keeping it in sealed, sterile containers. This process is still used today to keep milk free from germs. It is called pasteurization.

Pasteur married Marie Laurent of Strasberg, whom he loved deeply. She encouraged him always to put his laboratory first, and so he was able to concentrate on his work and do it well.

When little Joseph Meister was bitten fourteen times by a rabid dog and was brought to Louis Pasteur, the scientist hesitated to give his untried rabies vaccine to the boy. He did so only after two physicians pointed out that the boy would surely die without the vaccine, and that Pasteur just might have the answer.

Pasteur did have the answer, of course, and he saved Joseph Meister's life. Meister later became a gatekeeper at the Pasteur Institute. He stayed there, loyal to Louis Pasteur, for the rest of his life.

While Pasteur certainly believed in himself, he remained a quiet and humble man until his death in 1895. In his later years he was always a little amazed and amused by the fuss that people made over him. Once he accepted an invitation to attend an international medical meeting in London. When he arrived a steward asked him to come to the front of the assembly hall. Pasteur walked forward and the members rose to their feet and applauded. Pasteur seemed somewhat disappointed. "The Prince of Wales must be arriving," he said. "I wish we had arrived earlier so that we might gain a better view of him." But the chairman of the group only held out his hand to Pasteur. "No," he said. "It is you. It is you they are cheering."

The ValueTale Series

Great Gift Idea!

I Like to Read

The Value Tales Tote Bag! Designed exclusively for our Program, this sturdy vinyl tote bag is just the right size for favorite Value Tales books, and would make a perfect gift for any youngster in your life. The colorful tote, featuring the whimsical Dr. Values, can be yours for just $2.00, which *includes* shipping and handling! (New York and Connecticut residents must add sales tax.)

To order, simply send your name and complete address — remember to include your zip code — to the address below. Indicate the number of tote bags you wish us to send . . . they make delightful gifts! Allow 3 to 4 weeks for delivery.

 Grolier Enterprises Corp.

Dept. ZZ
SHERMAN TURNPIKE
DANBURY, CONNECTICUT 06816